ADVANCE PRAISE

"*The Baby Boomers kicked open the door to end of life conversations, Generation X kicked open the door to choices at end of life, and the Millennials have kicked open the door to the digital age. When combining the passion and zeal of these generations, we are now provided access, design, and choice at the end of life. Click Here When I Die is the bridge that connects all three generations' desires by pointing us to the essential elements: communication, choices that are available on demand, and documentation of end of life wishes on a digital platform. Together, we can change how individuals face end of life, access documented wishes anywhere, and perhaps even design it.*"

—KIMBERLY C. PAUL, AUTHOR, *DEATH BY DESIGN*

"Click Here When I Die is a must read for anyone who cares about their loved ones. Jon's story is compelling and fun to read. But even better, the reader also gets a simple process to follow. This makes it easy to get over the 'head trash' we have about doing the right thing and to plan to die responsibly instead of burying our heads in the sand. I highly recommend reading and sharing this book. Heck, buy it today. Before it's too late."

—CLIFFORD JONES, SON, HUSBAND, FATHER, ENTREPRENEUR, AND WRITER

"With his disarming sense of humor, Braddock tackles one of the most serious topics of our time: death. Anecdotes, including his own true story and life-changing lessons learned from the experiences of ordinary people create a real sense of urgency for anyone still breathing. Whether you're 25 or 105, this easy-to-digest, step-by-step guide will make you look like a prince when you're gone."

—JENNIFER BEBON, PRESIDENT/FOUNDER, MAX COMMUNICATIONS PR

"We all work too hard to see our money wasted, and we all say we love our family. Well, if you agree with both, then this book and the planning in it is for you. How do you want your loved ones to remember you?"

—CAMERON HEROLD, AUTHOR OF *DOUBLE DOUBLE* AND FATHER OF FOUR

"For the last seven and a half years, since my daughter was born, my wife and I have been putting off creating a Will and naming legal guardians for her if something should happen to us. Finally, the message Jon shares in his book was just what we needed to see in order to do what we knew was right all along. In a process that was far quicker and easier than we ever imagined, we created our Will online and named legal guardians. Since then, we've both enjoyed the peace of mind in knowing that those things are taken care of. Next in line—getting our digital house in order!"

—DAVID C., HUSBAND, FATHER, FREELANCE EDITOR, AND TECHNICAL COMMUNICATOR

CLICK HERE WHEN I DIE

JONATHAN S. BRADDOCK

CLICK HERE

WHEN I DIE

Making Things Easier for Those You Love

CLICK HERE WHEN I DIE

Making Things Easier for Those You Love

ISBN   978-1-61961-654-1 *Hardcover*

978-1-61961-610-3 *Paperback*

978-1-61961-611-0 *Ebook*

LIONCREST
PUBLISHING

This book is dedicated to Michelle—my wife, best friend, and business partner—for her strength, patience, and persistence in such a difficult time of pain and challenges, which was truly remarkable. It is only through her inspiration, advice, and belief in me, that this book was made possible. It is my hope that those reading these pages will be motivated to become thoughtfully prepared for the inevitable and will save their families from an inordinate amount of stress and time.

CONTENTS

INTRODUCTION

"Life does not cease to be funny when people die any more than it ceases to be serious when people laugh."

—GEORGE BERNARD SHAW

You are going to die!

Okay, now that I've got your attention, let's face facts... *You are still going to die!*

There's no getting around it. In fact, for the past three hundred thousand years since humans have been on this Earth, statistically one out of every one of us has died. I don't have an exact source for my statistic, but I'm pretty sure of its accuracy based on my own diligent research and personal observations.

A word of caution before we go any further: this book is intended only for people who fall into that category. In other words, if you're not going to die, feel free to put it down and grab the latest whodunit from James Patterson or the most recent incarnation of Harry Potter, if that's your thing. However, if you're one of the "100-percenters" of people who are going to die someday, then you should read this, because I'm going to teach you some invaluable information about this seemingly harsh reality.

This book is going to teach you all about the New Death Etiquette and how to be thoughtfully prepared for your own passing. You'll also understand that it doesn't have to be such a taboo topic, because it's okay to talk about death. In fact, it's healthy and necessary, and sometimes it can even be a little humorous. So, lighten up, it's only death!

THE OLD AND THE NEW DEATH ETIQUETTE

Start learning about the New Death Etiquette by asking yourself how you want to be remembered. Most of us want to ensure that we're leaving the correct legacy behind, that we're being thought of in the way we want to be thought of, rather than as inconsiderate, unprepared, self-absorbed, and delusional knuckleheads. We've already established that we're all going to die someday. The good news is that it's really not that scary, and preparing for it doesn't have to be all doom and gloom either, because it happens to roughly 6,775 people every day in the United States alone and approximately 154,889 people worldwide. So, get over yourself, and start thinking about how to make it easier on the people you leave behind. Ask yourself what you want life to be like for those around you who are still living it after you're gone.

Do you want them to have the time they need to properly mourn your loss, celebrate your life, forever reminisce about fond memories of the good times you were part of, and be able to move on with their own lives?

Or, do you want them to delay the healthy grieving of your loss because they're too busy trying to sort out the emotional, financial, and functional big, hot mess you left behind? Because without planning at least a little, that's exactly what's going to happen.

In 1971, it was possible to die peacefully in the United States without much concern over the order in which you left the remnants of your life. That is not the case in today's fast-paced, multitasking, social-media-driven society. Today, you have a plethora of online services, user IDs and passwords, insurance policies, financial accounts, online and offline memberships, and much more to consider.

Life is much easier and far more convenient today, because we can do such things as find a great place to eat right from a device we keep in our pockets at all times, even on a family vacation. Not to mention that it's also our camera now, with every waking moment of our lives fully documented without the need or expense of photo processing as in days gone by. It's a wonderful convenience to have, but what happens to all the valuable information stored in that device after we die? My digital photo album has in excess of four thousand pictures in it—none of which are in a pastel-colored, three-ring binder taking up valuable real estate on my coffee table at home.

We have a gazillion different television channels to choose from. Some of them may be paid for automatically from an online account or a periodic bank withdrawal from a joint account. What if your spouse doesn't use that service? Is he or she going to keep paying for something they don't use or want after you die?

All these conveniences have added up to an overwhelming level of complexity for our loved ones to unravel after we're gone. Most of us today have several online accounts, club memberships, subscriptions, life insurance policies, unclaimed money, and much more that nobody else even knows about. Or, maybe your spouse knows about it, but what happens if both of you are tragically taken at the same time in an accident? Who will figure it out in that event?

There's approximately a one-in-five-thousand chance that your cause of death will be from a car crash. I don't mean to be an alarmist, but that could happen anytime you get behind the wheel; it doesn't matter if you're seventy-five, fifty-five, or even twenty-five years old. In fact, after witnessing the way many people in their early twenties and late teens drive, I suspect that it's probably much more likely at that age.

Comparatively, there's about a one-in-eleven-million chance of dying in a plane crash and a one-in-thirty-two-million chance of winning Powerball.

The lesson learned from these statistics is the following:

Buckle up, don't be afraid to fly, and give the two dollars you'd spend on a Powerball ticket to a homeless person instead, because your odds of winning it are still almost just as good.

What this all means is that the life you leave behind today is much more complex than it used to be even twenty-five years ago. If Emily Post were alive today, she would be writing something about the differences between the Old and the New Death Etiquette.

Old School Death Etiquette: Dying any time before the widespread use of the Internet, computers, and other modern technologies basically meant that your loved ones needed to know how to dispose of your body, where to send the flowers, and how to address the thank-you cards for the massive amount of food that would arrive from every blood relative within a fifty-mile radius. Why people think lasagna is an effective way to grieve is still a bit of a mystery to me, but it's an unexplainable tradition in almost any culture to bring large amounts of heavy, belly-busting food during times of bereavement.

The New Death Etiquette: This is the art and consideration of knowing how to be thoughtfully prepared for your own passing. It is the notion of making things easier for your loved ones by leaving clear and concise instructions in regard to your final wishes for funeral desires, as well as the location and access to all important documents and accounts. Furthermore, it includes identifying who should be responsible for carrying out your final wishes and ultimately settling all end-of-life affairs. Unfortunately, your survivors are still going to have to deal with several different forms of pasta, tuna casseroles, and other heavy meals from the many grieving aunts, uncles, nieces, nephews, cousins, and others throughout your extended family.

Implementing this new and improved idea of Death Etiquette ("Now featuring 50 percent faster grieving time and 50 percent less mess to leave behind"—at least that's the way I see the marketing pitch going) doesn't have to be a daunting Debbie Downer of a task either. It should be a marathon, not a sprint, because you don't have to do it all in one sitting. If you go through the process methodically but effectively and logically, it should become very easy to manage and keep updated for thoughtful preparedness. Ultimately, it's a very simple act of undying love that you leave for your family. By not making them worry about tying together all of your loose ends and tracking down untapped financial resources, you are giving them the gift of time to properly grieve your loss.

Death is inevitable, and people are going to be sad about it. There's nothing you can do about that. However, the next part is something you can control. You can eliminate for your loved ones the frustration and stress of the prolonged experience of dealing with your final wishes. The choice is yours.

Chapter 1

THE SCAVENGER HUNT

> *"Everybody's gotta have a little place for their stuff. That's all life is about—trying to find a place for your stuff."*
>
> —GEORGE CARLIN

I was born in 1961 and grew up in a small town called Medford, New Jersey. That's where my father and grandfather had an insurance business right on Main Street, where pretty much everything was in Medford. There was a bank, a grocery store, and a post office—all right down the street. The town itself provided a fairly typical American background for my fairly typical American family. It's also the location of my first career endeavor as a young boy delivering the town newspaper, which was called the *Courier Post*.

Part of my job as newspaper delivery boy was to go to all the houses on my route every Friday night and collect the money for the newspaper and my delivery services. I had this green receipt book with small, spiral rings that held all the receipts together at the top. Most people would pay me by check, and I would give them a receipt so they could be sure that the delivery service would continue. Then I would stuff all the checks and receipt copies into an envelope and give them to the person who dropped off the stacks of newspapers at my doorstep in the morning. The whole idea of this seems so archaic now, where everything is not only delivered electronically but also paid for the same way. But, that's just the way it was back then—a little less convenient but much simpler.

Credit cards weren't in widespread use yet, so just about everybody paid for everything by check. Most people had a physical checkbook that contained paper checks, deposit slips, and ledgers to be balanced at the end of every month. When you got paid on Thursday or Friday, you went to the bank with that checkbook and deposited your weekly pay like every other working Joe in the country. In a lot of ways, this was a pretty great system, because there was always an easy paper trail to follow. If something happened to you and someone needed that information, chances were that you had that bank account information locked away in a desk drawer, lockbox, or hidden under a loose floorboard somewhere in the house. There was no online banking account with sophisticated cryptographic security involved that would lock your grieving loved one out after three failed attempts, and everyone in the family knew where the checkbook was hidden, just in case.

THE MORE THINGS CHANGE... THE MORE THINGS CHANGE

In the mid-1970s, the insurance business that my dad and grandfather owned was probably considered state of the art, because it was one of the first businesses I can remember that had a functioning computer system in it. It was this Jurassic-sized mainframe computer that had to be in an air-conditioned room at all times, or it would likely explode into a fiery, mushroom cloud of cathode ray tubes and various other Doctor Frankenstein–type electronic components. Funny thing is that I'm guessing the computing power packed in an iPhone of today is roughly fifty thousand times more powerful than that monstrosity.

To say that times have changed is a serious understatement.

Yes, we likely carry more computing power around in our pockets and on our wrists today than IBM had in their corporate headquarters back in 1971.

There is hardly ever a need to wait in line at the bank to cash or deposit a check anymore, because it's all done online in a cyber number crunch that takes place while we're sleeping safely in our beds at night.

The newspaper, or whatever is left of it, for many of us is delivered to our iPads and laptops every morning in a much neater, far more convenient and reliable electronic format. Best of all... no ink-stained fingers to lick while turning pages.

THEN AND NOW

Consider just how drastically some of the things we take for granted in our everyday lives have changed since 1971:

Then: All of your bills in 1971 would show up in paper form in the mailbox. Yes, the one that was in the front of your house or at the actual post office. Unfortunately, it was almost impossible to avoid them.

Now: E-bills have almost completely eliminated the need for paper billing. In fact, if you still choose paper billing, you're likely to draw the wrath of environmentalists everywhere, who desperately want you to save a tree or two by paying your bills entirely online. The only things that show up in my physical mailbox today are coupons for local pizza delivery shops and birthday cards from my mother.

Then: Television consisted of a piece of living room furniture that weighed roughly the same as a baby elephant. It had two dials on the front, and if you were lucky, you got a choice of about five channels to watch. One of them was usually PBS, and for most kids my age, that was a completely unacceptable choice, leaving you with four or fewer channels to choose from. That was okay, because chances were that *The Three Stooges*, *Looney Tunes*, or *Tom and Jerry* was on one of them.

Now: Cable or fiber-based television services provide us with somewhere around 999,999,999,999,999 channels, as well as the ability to watch almost any movie that's ever been made on demand for a small, one-time fee. We also have the ability to stream or download content to any device we carry with us, such as a smartphone, a tablet, or a laptop. Television is no longer relegated to the living room.

Then: In 1971, the Baltimore Colts beat the Dallas Cowboys 16–13 in Super Bowl V.

Now: Baltimore's football team is now known as the Ravens, who were once known as the Cleveland Browns. The Ravens were ultimately placed in Baltimore because the Colts moved to Indianapolis in the middle of the night. (Seriously, they packed up their belongings and took off under cover of darkness like a scorned lover.) The good news is that Cleveland eventually got their football team back and even kept their original name—the Browns. The bad news for their fans is that as of the time of this book, they still stink... badly. I guess some things actually don't change.

Then: Signaling System 1 had just been implemented by the old Bell System telephone companies. It was a revolutionary electronic switching system that allowed for such state-of-the-art features as call waiting and touch-tone dialing

Now: Not only is call waiting a feature we take for granted, but just like the Colts in Baltimore, the old Bell System telephone companies don't exist anymore.

Then: Acquiring information or doing research of any kind involved physically going to this strange building full of books called a public library. Once you got there, you either went straight for the reference section, where you tore through sections of the *Encyclopedia Britannica*, or you used your firm grasp of the Dewey Decimal System at the monolithic-looking device called a card catalogue to look up possible matches for books that *might* (if you were either tremendously lucky or really good at research) contain the information you needed. This resulted in your requested information being retrieved in roughly two to three hours, depending on how effective your use of the card catalogue was and whether or not you were able to make readable copies of the printed pages. It's no wonder we hated to do our homework so much.

Now: Google it! Information is retrieved in roughly two to three seconds. Then it can easily be cut, copied, and pasted directly into any paper or report. Strangely, my kids still hate doing homework! They laugh at me when I tell them that if we had Google when I was a kid, I would have gotten all A's, or at least I wouldn't have needed to forge my parent's signature on my report cards as much.

Then: Purchasing something involved walking into an actual store (likely Sears or K-Mart), finding the item you wanted, waiting in line, and purchasing it (most likely with cash).

Now: Type "amazon.com" in the address bar of your computer's browser, search for your desired item, click **Add to Cart**, and wait two business days for it to show up on your front doorstep. Soon, the need to leave your house may completely disappear. I really can't tell you when the last time was that I left my house to do Christmas or even birthday shopping, but it has been several years at least.

Then: The Ford Pinto was actually being purchased by thousands of Americans in 1971. It went on to achieve legendary status as one of the worst cars ever made, providing a horribly uncomfortable ride and serious, often life-threatening mechanical problems for anyone unlucky enough to own one of these überlemons.

Now: Cars almost drive themselves today... Wait a second—cars do drive themselves today! Companies such as Google and Uber have entire fleets of these things just waiting to take over the highways of America and the rest of the world. In fact, it's quite possible that kids being born today may never know what it's like to actually drive a car.

Times have definitely changed!

DEATH HITS CLOSE TO HOME

My father-in-law, Ted, passed away on September 2, 2013. It was Labor Day and also his sixty-third wedding anniversary with my mother-in-law, Marie. He died on his bedroom floor on an otherwise beautiful, sunny day in

Wisconsin. My wife, Michelle, and I were playing golf and approaching the fourth fairway when we got the phone call. It was one of those calls that you never forget. We left the balls wherever they were, turned the cart around, and immediately headed for home.

We were at my in-laws' house, which was not too far from our own, in under forty-five minutes. The local police and the medical examiner were there, and in the midst of this tragically acute case of shock at the loss of Michelle's father, she and I were being asked all these questions that we were totally unprepared for:

Police officer: "What funeral home should we take him to?"

Michelle and I: "We have no idea. Can you recommend a good one?"

Police officer: "Did he want to be buried or cremated?"

Michelle and I: "Seriously... um, yeah. We should probably figure that out, eh?"

Meanwhile, Michelle was understandably trying to collect herself and grasp the reality of what had just happened and console her grieving mother at the same time. Nobody is really prepared or even remotely capable of thoughtfully answering those questions at a time like that.

During that time, someone starts telling your loved ones about all the things that need to get done:

- They have to put together an obituary.
- They have to plan a funeral or memorial service.
- They will probably want to gather photos for a memory board.
- They need to decide on burial or cremation arrangements.
- They have relatives to call.
- There's life insurance for them to collect.
- Someone has to pay the funeral home.
- They need to call your workplace and let them know what happened.
- And, a few dozen other decisions that need to be made *now*.

The list is seemingly endless, and they just hope they're making the right decisions on the spot. People are barking directives at them, and it's all like a surreal scene out of a Francis Ford Coppola movie, where the sound is muffled in the background and they're just staring at their surroundings with dizzying emotions and blurred awareness. It's not a realistic expectation for anyone to be able to correctly make any sort of reasonable arrangements at that particular time. That's one reason why it's enormously helpful to the people you care about to have it all written down somewhere. That way, all they need to remember is where you put those instructions for this undeniable fate for all of humanity. When the police were asking us all those questions, Michelle and I would have just needed to be coherent enough to tell them where to find the document that had all the answers they needed.

HONEY, I HAVE SOME BAD NEWS

There were massive amounts of boxes to go through, because Ted was a borderline hoarder. Okay, maybe he wasn't a clinical hoarder, but he sure had a lot of *stuff.* Ted probably thought he was well organized, and for all intents and purposes, he was. The problem was that he failed to tell anyone where the encryption key to his *Da Vinci Code* for finding any of it was. He had a home office that was probably about 120 square feet. It had a chair and a desk in it with three or four filing cabinets jammed full of documents. The desk drawers were also spilling over with more documents—canceled checks, bank statements, and all kinds of business papers dating back to the '60s and '70s. Not only were the filing cabinets and desk drawers bursting at the seams, but there were also boxes stacked on top of more boxes on the floor and an entire closet full of... more boxes! That office was one big clusterf**k of clutter—maybe we should combine the terms into one more descriptive, all-encompassing word, and call it a clutterf**k?

Finally, a couple of weeks after digging through a seemingly endless pile of papers, we resurrected the Will from one of those boxes. And after looking through it, we found some startling information. I said, "Honey, I've got some bad news. After looking at your dad's Will, I'm afraid you're going to live with your Aunt Jean and Uncle Ed in Milwaukee from now on. Sorry, hon, but apparently, that's what your dad wanted." Being X years old (Hey, a gentleman never reveals his wife's age), Michelle found this quite the revelation!

If this had been an Adam Sandler movie, somehow Michelle would have been legally bound to move in with her aunt and uncle, and plenty of potty humor and slapstick-style hilarity would ensue for roughly ninety minutes—or however long the average moviegoer could stand it. Fortunately, that's not the way the real world works. Michelle got to stay with our family, and Uncle Ed and Aunt Jean didn't have to clear out the spare bedroom to make room for her. Nonetheless, she and Marie spent weeks digging through the mess, trying to uncover an updated Will, but no such document existed.

Ted died at the age of eighty-eight and apparently hadn't updated his Will since 1962. Kudos to the man for having the initial awareness to take care of things back when Michelle had just been a child, but things change. Having a last Will and Testament is a critically important part of the New Death Etiquette, but it doesn't end there. You need to keep it updated.

Truthfully, I'm not sure we ever actually uncovered all of Ted's *stuff.* It was like a massive jigsaw puzzle with missing pieces. You open the box back up, get 90 percent through putting it together, and then realize there are still two or three pieces missing. To this day, there is still probably some unclaimed life insurance out there for him. Unfortunately, the only one who knows about it isn't around to say anything—so easy come, easy go, I suppose.

MY ENTREPRENEURIAL NATURE KICKS IN: IDENTIFY THE PROBLEM AND CREATE A SOLUTION

Three weeks after Ted passed away, I found myself in the backyard by the pool with a cigar in my mouth, which just happens to be one of my favorite ways to sit back and relax. I know all about the dangers of this bad habit, but heck, I know all about the New Death Etiquette too, so at least I have that going for me if and when enjoying these things finally kills me. The problem was that I had been engaging in this *alone time* a lot in those three weeks, because my wife was going up the street every night to where her parents lived, helping Marie sort through the mass of *stuff* my father-in-law had left behind. I could have gone over there to help out, but I felt like it wasn't really my place. It seemed more like a mother-daughter thing, and I didn't want to get in the way.

As I was sitting by the pool, basking in my own disturbingly familiar self-indulgence once again, I had a thought: I grabbed my iPad and immediately went to the Notability application. In 1971, I would have reached for a piece of paper and a crayon or whatever was available to write with. That may have involved something as remarkably inconvenient as physically getting up to go find a writing instrument in the house, which would have severely diminished the value of my current Zen-like state of mind. Thank God (or Brahma, Ahura Mazda, or whatever other supreme deity you choose to recognize) for the iPad.

STUFF

It occurred to me that if something were to happen to Michelle and me, our kids wouldn't have the slightest idea of where to begin. I began writing down all this *stuff* that my wife was telling me they were going through—financial accounts, retirement plans, personal belongings, assorted memorabilia, Social Security letters, bank statements, insurance information, military documentation, and much more. Some people refer to this collection of *stuff* as their estate. Those people would refer to their

Will as an estate plan. In layman's terms, an estate plan is nothing more than a document that explains where all your *stuff* goes after you die. You don't need to live in a mansion with a butler and a chauffeur-driven limousine behind iron gates to have an estate plan—you just need *stuff*... and we all have *stuff.*

My next thought was, *What if I had a workbook that itemized everything they were rooting through?* I began writing more and more things—online accounts, passwords and user IDs, social media permissions, information on pets, last wishes, legal advisors, tax records, and more still. By the time I was done writing, I had come up with about ten sections of this workbook.

It blew me away that there was so much *stuff* in our lives to consider after we die. It doesn't matter whether you're a sixty-year-old housekeeper or Bill Gates—you've got plenty of *stuff.* You don't have to be a billionaire to have a Netflix account with autopay that nobody will know how to shut off unless you have the password written down somewhere. You don't need to be rich to have a lot of things today. Heck, there are plenty of people in America living off government assistance that have the latest version of the iPhone with unlimited data and texting. You don't need to be rich or even financially secure to have a lot of *stuff* anymore.

George Carlin was a comic legend in his lifetime who did an epic comedy bit on the idea of *stuff*. It's actually one of his most famous bits, and it just happens to be even more poignant for our consideration now that he's passed. Why? Because currently, his daughter, Kelly, is in charge of his estate—or his *stuff*—which supposedly contains everything from scrapbooks to handwritten jokes, marked-up scripts, and even arrest records. All that *stuff* now sits in a place called the National Comedy Center in Jamestown, New York (not so coincidentally, the hometown of Lucille Ball), where fans of Carlin's one-of-a-kind dry wit and infectious candor can go see it all.

Just imagine if Carlin's daughter hadn't known how to find his *stuff*. Or, what if she hadn't been aware that her father's final wishes were to have his *stuff* on display somewhere? This treasure trove of personal memorabilia and his professional legacy wouldn't be available for his admirers and fans to take in. Now Carlin's legendary status can justifiably live on in the world of comedy greatness forever.

I don't know how long it took Kelly Carlin to go through her father's *stuff*, but it took Michelle and Marie several months to go through all of Ted's, and none of it was so undeniably valuable that it was going to a museum of any kind. The silver lining, however, is that it did cause to me to create this workbook based on all of the things they discovered. After I took a really good look at what I created, I had another thought: *Shit, what if my father-in-law had just been a little more organized and had the locations of all his stuff documented somewhere?* Maybe it would have taken them a few days, or a week at the most, to go through it all, and I wouldn't be sitting alone by the pool every night contributing so often to my own progressive form of lip, tongue, gum, or lung cancer. Then I started looking around online, but I couldn't find anything else quite like this workbook. So, I decided to print it, and I still have that original copy today. Maybe that can go to a museum someday... Later, I took that printout and gave it to our marketing person, Jenny. I asked her if we could make a professional-looking version of the workbook out of the printout and give it to our clients.

THE *MY LIFE AND WISHES ORGANIZER* IS BORN

Voilà! That workbook became the first draft of the *My Life and Wishes Organizer*, which we self-published and which still sells on Amazon today in a much more refined and comprehensive format. We started taking it to the clients of our employee benefit consulting company. At most of the sites we visited, the chief human resources officer was absolutely blown away when we showed it to them. Because the vast majority of them had personally experienced or witnessed the time-consuming mess that was left behind following the death of a loved one, they would say something like, "Wow, can we buy one of these for our people?" In my own head, I was thinking something like, *Wow, I was going to just give it to you, but if you want to buy it—what the hell? Cool!*

Before I knew it, I had all kinds of clients coming to me, asking to buy these things. As the organizer got increasingly popular, I had another realization, which was that everybody who has one of them also needs a really good number-2 pencil with an eraser, because as we mentioned earlier, things change—passwords, insurance policies, caretaker designations, pets, doctors, friends, valuables—everyone's *stuff* changes over time, more than most of us think it would.

The next logical progression for this invention was to take it online, so that's what I did. I spent the next eighteen months and an awful lot of investment capital working with developers, programmers, and other very talented specialists to build a superior online platform for my organizer, which also happens to be a heck of a lot more secure than any online banking platform.

SIDE EFFECTS OF THE SCAVENGER HUNT

Michelle and I were fortunate in one way when her father passed, because we own our own business. Therefore, we could take all the time off from work that we needed to make phone calls and chase down financial accounts and insurance policies without getting in trouble with the boss. Other people—employers—aren't going to be so keen on your grieving loved ones taking two to three hours off work every day to call these places to sort out all of your *stuff*. It all contributes to the most common and most serious side effect of the scavenger hunt, which is stress. I can only imagine how much this is amplified when the loved one was out of town or even lived in another state!

It's not just about stress in the workplace either; the scavenger hunt creates stress in the home as well. Your loved ones' entire family enters survival mode. They're spending an inordinate amount of time dealing with logistical arrangements and final wishes, as well as locating lost items and unclaimed accounts, so they unwittingly begin to forget about or even ignore some of the very important matters of their own everyday life. They put off the usual productive conversations with their kids at dinnertime, forget to pay the bills that keep the heat and lights on, and even stop eating right because they've just got too much on their mind, too much unpleasantness to deal with, and way too much leftover lasagna from their aunt Gertrude.

Another unfortunate side effect is that they don't have time to grieve properly. Chasing down all those loose ends causes them to have to put off what is likely the most important process in your death, which is healing. There's so much to do that they just sort of walk around on autopilot. They don't have time to really grasp it, accept it, and move on, so they just walk around like a zombie from *The Walking Dead*. Rather than healing, they end up just trying to get through another day and hopefully tie up one or more loose ends in the process.

OUR LIVES CONSIST OF A MILLION AND ONE TENTACLES

Our lives in the twenty-first century have a million and one tentacles of *stuff* attached. Even if you have lived what you might think of as a relatively mundane existence, you probably have a somewhat overwhelming level of complexity to your life experiences that will affect what you leave behind. Think about questions like:

- Who are you, and how do you want to be remembered?
- What city were you born in?
- Where have you lived?
- What high school did you attend?
- What college did you go to?
- Where have you worked?
- How long have you worked there?
- What have you accomplished personally and professionally?
- Do you belong to any fraternities from college?
- Do you belong to any organizations outside of school?
- What about other memberships?
- What websites do you have online accounts with?
- What about military experience?

The list goes on and on for most of us—probably enough to fill ten pages worth of questions, and there are consequences to each of them that you may not realize. For instance, there could be a school newspaper that wants to publicize your obituary. You may have fraternal brothers from college who want to be notified of your death, so they don't reach out to you via Facebook ten months later with an awkward post like, "Hey, Braddock, you antisocial son of a bitch! Where have you been lately? Are you too good to talk to your brothers at Delta House these days? Blutarsky's pissed!" Pardon me for the subtle homage to *Animal House*, but you get the point.

In the case of my father-in-law, one of the tentacles in his life included a small VA benefit from his four-year stint in World War II that we were able to claim. The problem was that we didn't realize this until at least a couple of months after his passing, so it didn't do anything to help with his funeral expenses. Conversely, if he just had this *stuff* written down somewhere, we would have been able to locate such things as mysterious keys, insurance policies, and VA benefits much more quickly and much less painstakingly.

Don't underestimate the many tentacles of your digital life either. Access privileges to your digital life definitely need to be written down somewhere. Most of us today have online accounts at numerous online service providers, such as Netflix, Hulu, LinkedIn, Facebook, Twitter, YouTube, Amazon, Bank of America, Express Scripts, and so on. You should have passwords written down for all these sites anyway. Then, all you need to do is make sure somebody knows where you have those passwords written down, so they can more easily cancel accounts when you die.

Writing down the various places you've lived is also an underrated matter of importance. Modern society is a world full of nomads. We move from place to place, depending on jobs, spouses, children, weather, school systems, and more. Personally, I was born in New Jersey and lived there until I was fourteen years old, but I've also lived in New Hampshire, Colorado, Oklahoma, and, most recently, Wisconsin. Previously, I conducted an online search for unclaimed money and actually found something with my name on it in Oklahoma. Not to sound like a radio advertisement for one of these services, but "there may be unclaimed money out there with your name on it." Sadly, there are likely millions of dollars in unclaimed money out there for people who are no longer breathing. Even if you have no intention of using one of those online services to look into this matter for yourself, at least make it possible for your kids to locate it after you're gone. Maybe it's not even a matter of unclaimed money; maybe it's more about them being able to tell a story a little more completely about who you were and where you've been in your life. Either way, it's all part of the million and one tentacles that you use to reach out to people and places throughout your life, and they could all become important to someone after you're gone.

Chapter 2

TALK ISN'T CHEAP

*"I wish I'd known Mom wanted to be
cremated before I buried her."*

—MY FRIEND AND ESTEEMED COLLEAGUE, NICK BERARD

When I was growing up, there were four things that nobody ever talked about. There was an unwritten rule that you just didn't talk about politics, religion, money, or death. Politics and religion were so controversial that if you talked to someone with a different point of view, you may have started a holy war that you never intended. Money was never discussed, because it was in bad taste (poor life etiquette) to talk about how much money you made. For instance, I never knew what my parents earned when I was a child.

Those subjects aren't as taboo today as they were in previous decades, though. For instance, most of us are all too willing to start a holy war about politics or religion if somebody has the unmitigated ignorance to disagree with our own painfully clear and obviously correct point of view... right? Talking politics and religion these days is not only okay, it's expected. People want to know if you're a Democrat, Republican, Libertarian, Christian, Buddhist, Hindu, pagan, or Scientologist. They want to know about it mostly because they want to be able to debate you on it and show you why you're wrong. Money—everybody talks about money now. Gordon Gecko from the movie *Wall Street* and his "Greed is good" mantra of the '80s changed all that. We live in a society of dual-income households, and today's generation spends money like no other. The economy is a global issue now, too, so making money is an even more acceptable talking point worldwide. After all, it's only money.

THE MYTH OF THE SELF-FULFILLING PROPHECY

Death, however, is still something that hardly anybody besides a mortician wants to talk about. It's as if the mere act of talking about it is going to have some sort of prophetic effect. This phenomenon, however, makes no sense at all, because we love talking about sex, and that doesn't make us pregnant. So, does a buzzer go off at the Grim

Reaper's house every time someone talks about death? Just picture him sitting in his recliner with a bowl of nachos in his bony lap while watching *America's Got Talent* as he sighs disgustedly because his death buzzer went off again. He probably gets up, shuts the clicker, grabs his scythe, and heads out the door to go collect his next overly chatty, unfortunate human soul.

The subject of death is still so taboo that it's also the one thing you likely shy away from talking about with your kids. You do your best to teach them about such things as having good manners and being respectful to others. Then you talk to them about peer pressure, and when they get a little older, you may even discuss sex with them, which is something previous generations *never* talked about. But death is still something you avoid discussing with them until maybe their pet hamster finally has a tragic accident on his running wheel while infinitely chasing a piece of cheese and dies of a heart attack. Even then, you might just sweep him out of the cage really fast and tell your kids that he ran away before they experience the traumatic visual of seeing his petrified hamster corpse in his cage.

DEATH AND TAXES

It's especially odd that you don't talk about death, because it's definitely going to happen. My firm used an East Coast survey company to conduct a national survey in January 2016 that covered many different areas concerning death. One of the questions was "Why haven't you planned or talked about end-of-life planning?" Some of the responses were as follows, with my responses to them below each:

"I'm not ready to, because I haven't made any decisions."

So, you haven't decided whether you will die or not yet?

"I'm afraid. I think it's bad luck to talk about death."

Just because we talk about something doesn't mean it's going to happen. After all, how many times do we talk about winning the lottery?

"I'm too busy."

If you're really that busy, then it's even more important that you make end-of-life preparations, because being busy means you've got a lot of stuff to sort out.

"I'll do it later—when it needs to be done."

Just before you bleed out? Hey, wake-up... later may be too late!

"It's too uncomfortable and depressing. It's not something I want to talk about unless I have to."

Newsflash: You have to.

"My life and affairs are complicated."

All the more reason to make sure the ones you love aren't stuck trying to sort out the big hot mess of your life after you're gone.

"My life and affairs are fairly simple and straightforward."

It's probably far more complex than you realize, especially if you have financial accounts, life insurance, and online activity.

"I don't want to start a fight. I hate to rock the boat."

Don't rock the boat while you're alive, and don't be around when you die and it capsizes?

"It's just not particularly important to me."

Selfish much?

That last response must have been from the male demographic, because until we reach about thirty years old, most of us boys think we're immortal. Death is for old people, and evidently women, because since we've launched our Facebook site, over 85 percent of our engagement is females over the age of forty. Part of this is probably because women live an average of seven years longer than men, so they're a little more likely to be the ones left to figure everything out. Another reason is probably that women just tend to be more detail-oriented than most men.

Bear with me while I take a sidebar here. By nature, we're all planners—men and women—we plan for everything.

We make a list to go to the grocery store and determine which roads we will take to avoid traffic on the way.

We plan what we want to do over the weekend. We plan what we will wear on that special date.

We plan for anniversaries, birthday parties, weddings, births, graduations, vacations, our retirement, and we even plan what we are going to have for dinner and what we will watch on TV later tonight. Why is that?

I think it's because planning for those things are fun—they bring us joy and happiness. Yes, that sort of planning is self-directed for our own benefit (dare I say a little selfish). But most of us don't want to think about or plan for our own death, because it brings us no joy or happiness.

In general, we simply don't do this type of planning because it doesn't do anything for us. Hell, we'll be gone, right? Let me state the obvious, planning for our own inevitable passing isn't done for us; it is done for others and it is outwardly directed. It is done out of selfless care, concern, and love for those we leave behind.

THE CONVERSATION

It's not fun to talk about death—I get it. We'd all rather talk about much nicer things, such as vacations in the Bahamas, puppies, and YouTube videos featuring babies doing ridiculously cute things, but you can save your spouse and the rest of your family so much aggravation by having a realistic conversation about what to do after you die. You don't need to talk about it over and over again—just once is all you need—and it doesn't have to be all doom and gloom either. You can keep it light. The conversation may sound something like this:

"Honey, there are a couple of things you need to know. First, I have documented everything you'll need to know when I'm no longer here, and this is where you'll find it. (Up to you where you put it—could be in your sock drawer, or anywhere you see fit.) Second, we live in a three-thousand-square foot house with two and a half acres of green grass to mow, three feet of snow to shovel every winter, a leaking roof, and twelve rooms that need to be regularly cleaned. If I die first, please sell the goddamned thing! Downsize into a nice condo where they mow the lawn, shovel the sidewalk, and maybe even deliver your mail to the front door for you. If it's still too much to clean, take some money out of our savings and hire a maid service. There's no need for you to tackle all this upkeep, and it just doesn't make sense to burden the kids with it either, although it might be a nice payback for all those times they ignored us when we asked them to clean their rooms... But seriously, sell this beast and downsize—it's just a house. Memories are in your heart, not confined to a bunch of two-by-fours with windows. That's all, now... what shall we have for dinner?"

If you don't have that conversation before you die, you risk your spouse staying in a home they can't keep up with and maybe even trying to pay some bills they can't continue to afford, all because they think that is what you wanted them to do. Tell them to cash out the life insurance and move to Florida if that's what they want to do. There's no need for pride and misplaced sentiment to take over the remainder of their lifetime. Don't force your adult kids to take time away from their families to come shovel the sidewalks and trim the hedges of a house that your widow or widower can't possibly maintain because they foolishly think you would want it that way.

REMEMBERING 7 OR 8 OUT OF 860.3 MILLION *IS* A LOT TO ASK

Talking about death is a big step in the right direction. Writing it down after you talk about it is an even bigger and better step. To put it in terms that Neil Armstrong might use: "That's one small step for the New Death Etiquette and one giant step for my legacy." The good news is that talking about death isn't nearly as difficult as walking on the moon, but it's only good if somebody remembers what you said. For a deeper understanding of this, consider the following story of a friend and professional associate of mine, Nick Berard.

Nick is an amazing artist, brilliant photographer, and all-around awesome video guy who works with my company.

His mother was tragically killed at the young age of fifty-one in a head-on car accident caused by a drunk driver when Nick was just twenty-four years old. Nick got the worst call of his life in the middle of the night, and he found himself driving from Wisconsin to a hospital in Memphis, Tennessee, where his mom had been traveling on business. Unfortunately, Nick's sister had been estranged from his mother and proved to be no help in making any sort of arrangements. It's also worth noting that Nick's wife had just given birth. At his age, he already had plenty on his mind, so dealing with the sudden and tragic death of his mother all by himself was somewhat overwhelming.

There was Nick, just starting his new life with his beautiful family and trying to properly grieve the very sudden and tragic loss of his mother at the same time. Simultaneously, he was trying to make all these very adult decisions regarding her final wishes at a time in life when many of us are just leaving college, still eating pizza five nights a week, and trying to save enough scratch to buy a used car.

By hell or high water, Nick made all the necessary arrangements. Although he really had no idea what to do, he just took the advice of others and admirably did the best he could. Looking back on it today, Nick says he was in a complete fog at the time and listened to trusted friends and other family members who told him where to have the funeral and where to bury her, as well as how to deal with all the financial *stuff*, including the selling of her house. Ironically, Nick hadn't even bought a house for his own family yet.

It took a long time, but Nick eventually went through the whole process. About a year after the dust finally settled, Nick had somewhat of an unsettling recollection. Maybe things had finally settled down enough for him to have a moment of clarity, but he remembered his mother telling him not to waste his money on an expensive box and a big service for her body. She wanted him to just dispose of her and move on with his life. In other words, she preferred to be cremated, quick and easy, without him spending a lot of time and money on her final resting place. What a startling moment this was for him, because when his mother passed, he was in shock. He was completely unable to remember this seemingly innocuous conversation he had had with his mother about five years earlier, because he was so understandably overwhelmed at the time. Therefore, he just listened to what other people he trusted were telling him to do, which is also completely understandable.

Nick still thinks about this all the time. In fact, he visits his mother's grave in Milwaukee a few times every year, and he describes it as a completely impactful experience every time, knowing that his mother is buried there, but that's not what she really wanted.

History tends to rewrite itself over time, and your words and actions can thus get distorted or totally forgotten sometimes. You say a lot of words throughout your life—860.3 million of them (give or take a few thousand), according to *The Joy of Lex: How to Have Fun with 860,341,500 Words* by self-proclaimed word expert Gyles Brandreth. Interestingly enough, this number equates to roughly the entire content of both the Old and New Testaments of the King James Bible more than a whopping one thousand times! Do the math, and by age twenty-four, Nick had likely heard somewhere around 275 million words. Therefore, to highlight the importance of letting people know what your final wishes are, I ask you this:

How the hell would Nick remember a mere seven or eight words spoken by his mother from a day just like any other out of a possible 275 million?

If you have loved ones and you truly want the best for them after you're gone, have a conversation and write it down.

A PERMANENT VACATION

When you go on vacation for more than just a long weekend, you probably have a friend or neighbor take care of a few things around the house while you're gone. As a result, you have a conversation with the appointed home caretaker. This conversation usually involves giving them several key pieces of information, such as the following:

- Here's how often to let the dog out and what food to feed him.
- Here's how to take care of the fish tank.
- Here are the codes to the security system and instructions for using it.
- Here's where we keep the spare keys.
- Be sure to water the plants.
- Take in the mail.
- Here's my contact info: use it if you have any questions.
- Whatever you do, *don't* investigate that strange smell coming from underneath the floorboards. (Seriously, if there's a place in the house that you don't feel comfortable with others being in for whatever reason, tell them it's off limits and lock it up.)

The list is probably much larger, but that's a good start. The point is that you always have a conversation with your house sitter when you go on vacation. Why don't you have the same conversation with someone about the time you go on a permanent vacation? House-sitting requires clear and concise instructions, and death is no different. Someone still needs to take care of what you leave behind, but instead of doing it for a week or two, they need to permanently take care of it.

KEEP IT SHORT AND SWEET

You don't need to set aside a three-hour video conference call with your spouse and all your adult kids with their families to talk about what should happen after the Grim Reaper inevitably comes for you. In fact, I suggest exactly the opposite: limit your audience to your spouse and one responsible older child, trustworthy friend, or professional advisor, and keep the conversation short and sweet. You don't need to tell everybody where the family plot is or anything else. There's no need to include all the gory details in the conversation, such as finances, insurance policies, old college roommates to notify, and access privileges. Just make sure it's all written down somewhere, and tell somebody where to find the master document.

By limiting the conversation, you remove some of the doom and gloom associated with the subject. It should last only five or ten minutes, and then everybody can go on with the rest of their lives without feeling overly downtrodden for the rest of the day. What's imperative is that you tell these few trusted and responsible individuals where the documentation is that spells out every last detail of your final wishes. The conversation itself can be as simple as the following:

"Look, we're all going to die someday. The good news is that we have no idea when it's going to happen. When that day comes for me, here's what you need to know. Go into my top dresser drawer in my bedroom—on the right side, underneath the socks. You'll find an envelope. In that envelope, you'll find everything you need to know. It will provide answers to all your questions and instructions for my final wishes and more."

The *My Life and Wishes* service is great, because it's very comprehensive, online-accessible, easily modified, and totally secure, but it's also fine if you want to do it differently. You can just buy an old spiral ring notebook and a number-2 pencil from the drugstore, write everything down, and keep the notebook someplace safe. Once again, make sure you have a good eraser, because that information will change periodically.

Chapter 3

PROACTIVITY OVER PROCRASTINATION

"*Procrastination is the bad habit of putting off until the day after tomorrow what should have been done the day before yesterday.*"

—NAPOLEON HILL, AUTHOR

The New Death Etiquette strongly encourages proactivity in place of procrastination, especially if you have aging parents. Horrible conditions such as Alzheimer's and dementia rob people of their faculties and render them incapable of making good decisions. That's why it's important as the adult child of an aging parent that you have the conversation before it's too late. If they're not able or willing to write down the vital information concerning their end-of-life affairs, then you need to have that conversation with them and write it down for them—the sooner, the better.

PROACTIVITY IN ACTION

Sadly, early-onset Alzheimer's can happen much sooner in life than people realize. Consider the following story of a woman named Julie, her sister-in-law Rose, and Rose's daughter April.

Rose, a divorced single mother of one daughter, was a fifty-seven-year-old vibrant woman, seemingly with a lot of life left to live. However, in December 2014, she was diagnosed with early-onset Alzheimer's, and a whirlwind of emotions followed.

Shortly thereafter, Rose took early retirement and voluntarily surrendered her driver's license—both remarkably selfless and intelligent decisions for someone whose entire world had just come crashing down on her. Her daughter April would become her caregiver, because they always had a special relationship—inseparable to the very end.

One day, Rose's sister-in-law Julie received a call from her, asking her to become her second power of attorney (POA). Julie's acceptance of this responsibility gave Rose a feeling of comfort and reassurance, because she didn't want to overwhelm April with her care and all of her responsibilities.

First, the three of them created a list of what needed to be tackled right away. Realizing that time was of the essence, Rose, April, and Julie teamed up to accomplish all they could before Alzheimer's would take it all away from them. They quickly got the POA documents signed for financial and healthcare purposes, which instilled an immediate sense of relief for Rose. Then, they went to the Aging and Disability Resource Center (ADRC), which is a program provided by the State Department of Health Services in Rose's home state of Wisconsin. Its purpose is to help people with disabilities enroll in Medicaid and other similar programs so they can receive the care they need.

Alzheimer's moved almost as fast as the terrific trio could straighten out Rose's affairs for her. They had enrolled Rose in ADRC in March 2015, but it took almost a full year, February 2016, to finally get everything squared away. In the ensuing ten months, Rose's disease had progressed from moderate to severe. The healthcare POA had to be activated, because Rose became unable to make decisions anymore. Fortunately, Rose, April, and Julie were proactive rather than procrastinating in this case; they had the necessary conversations and knew what to do each step of the way as Rose's Alzheimer's progressed further.

The moral of the story: be proactive, because death, much like time, waits for no one.

DON'T WAIT FOR A WAKE-UP CALL

Procrastination is a demon, totally capable of undermining the productive nature of even the most productive souls of humanity. Most of us understand that we're going to die someday, that there's a need to make arrangements, but few of us regard this need as something that can't wait a year or two... or twenty. Then, some of us get a wake-up call—it could be a scare with a health condition or a near-miss car accident. Sadly, it's only after that wake-up call that some of us realize how quickly life can change, or end, in the blink of an eye. One minute, you're doing your best *Carpool Karaoke* impression while driving seventy miles per hour down the highway, screaming the lyrics and playing air guitar to a classic '80s tune, and the next minute, you're hydroplaning across three lanes of traffic, seemingly in slow motion while your life flashes in front of your eyes. Don't wait for the wake-up call. Be proactive, and get your *stuff* organized today.

Dan is a friend of mine in his mid-thirties with small children. He was a little overweight and had some other health issues when he went to see his doctor one day. The doctor told him that he needed a heart procedure, and he needed it now. It wasn't one of those things where Dan could go home and discuss it with his wife and family for a few days. No, they took him to the hospital from the doctor's office, because his heart required immediate medical attention.

As Dan was preparing for surgery, he went through all the possibilities of what the future would bring in his own mind. It doesn't help any when the doctor brings out that lovely form that says something along the lines of "By the way, you could die; sign here."

Usually we expect everything in surgery rooms to go as planned, but every once in a while, something happens, and this realization brings you quickly in touch with your own mortality. So, Dan started writing down all his *stuff*—life insurance, bank accounts, where to find *stuff*, whom to call, and so on.

By the way, Dan is now the picture of health, along the lines of *American Ninja Warrior*. He is currently loving life with his family, and he also has everything planned out and in place for his passing (hopefully, fifty years or more from now).

The next story is more of the life-flashing-before-your-eyes variety, where there was no time to think about anything.

Derek is the husband of a nice woman who works with me. In fact, she's worked with me for over fifteen years. Derek was a tanker-truck driver who drove all around the state of Wisconsin. One snowy December morning, just before sunrise, a deer ran out from the approaching landscape of the dark and stormy back roads. Instinctively, Derek tried to steer the tanker away from the fleeting animal, but he lost control of the vehicle in the process, causing it to flip. Fortunately, it didn't explode, but Derek was trapped inside for a while. Much like Dan when he was waiting for surgery, Derek's mind began racing as he was waiting for a rescue crew to remove him from the vehicle. He started thinking about all the reasons he needed to stay alive—his wife and son being on the very top of that list.

Heart surgery in your thirties and a deer causing your vehicle to flip on a country back road aren't events all that uncommon. They happen all the time, which is why procrastination is not your friend. There's no need to dwell on this sort of thing—just be aware of it so you can get your preparation out of the way and never have to think about it again.

BETTER LATE THAN NEVER... SORT OF

I published the *My Life and Wishes Organizer* and gave a copy of it to my mother shortly after the following story happened. Her response to me was something like, "Oh great! If only you had done this a few years ago, how much easier would my life have been!"

My parents split half their time in the great white north of New Hampshire and the other half in sunny Florida. She had only one brother—a lifelong bachelor, who was also a bit of a nomad, dividing his time between the Jersey Shore, Long Beach Island, and a condo in Florida. Her brother was three years older than she was and died at the age of eighty, which means she was about seventy-seven at the time. They had had a few previous discussions about what to do after he died, because he had recently become very ill. He'd been in and out of the hospital for a while, and my mother had gone down to visit him whenever she could, but he'd never really wanted to talk too much about it because of his typical "Oh, I'll be fine" male bravado.

Luckily, she was able to get him to give her POA so she would at least have the legal capacity to take care of his estate after he died. The problem was that he never told her where anything was. So, my mother had to make frequent treks to New Jersey to attempt to straighten out his affairs, but my uncle Rob had a roommate, so she couldn't just stay at his place and take care of things all at once. She had to stay at the local Holiday Inn Express and coordinate trips with his roommate to dig through his *stuff*, while working with an attorney to help her navigate through all the inheritance taxes and other messes he had left behind.

She also had to spend time at his condo in Florida, sorting through things. Worst of all, both homes had to be sold, and Uncle Rob had never specified whether or not the property in New Jersey should be sold to his roommate. As it turned out, the roommate couldn't afford the property anyway, so the event dislodged another human being on top of all the mess my mother was dealing with.

The whole process of my seventy-seven-year-old mother settling Uncle Rob's final affairs took a little over two years before everything was sold, personal belongings were uncovered, attorneys and taxes were paid in both states, and all the living could get back to their lives.

Perhaps the saddest part of this story is that it isn't all that unique. It happens every day, not only across the country but around the world. Furthermore, it's 100 percent avoidable and the avoiding is not that difficult to accomplish.

Chapter 4

STAIRWAY TO HEAVEN

*"Yes, there are two paths you can
go by, but in the long run
There's still time to change the road you're on."*

—JIMMY PAGE, ROBERT PLANT

Thanks to rock legends Jimmy Page and Robert Plant, you're poetically reminded that there's still time to change your current path of inactivity regarding the New Death Etiquette. However, as you learned from Rose's story in the last chapter, life has a way of forcing unexpected changes on you rather quickly and without advance notice. Effectively implementing the New Death Etiquette involves a three-step process that I like to call the Stairway to Heaven.

STEP ONE: WHAT ARE YOUR FINAL WISHES?

The first step on the Stairway to Heaven is to let people know what your final wishes are by giving them the answers to such questions as the following:

- Do you want to be buried or cremated?
- If you desire a burial, where?
- Is there a specific plot somewhere?
- What kind of funeral do you want?
- Religious ceremony or nonreligious?
- Is there a certain church you prefer?
- Which of the pastors or priests do you want to preside over your service?
- Do you want a small family gathering graveside?
- Do you want a wake or not?
- If you prefer cremation, what do you want us to do with the ashes?

Would you like us to leave a donation to the American Cancer Society in your remembrance? How about the American Heart Association, Alzheimer's Foundation, or the Boys & Girls Clubs of America?

I've explained to my wife that I've already attended more wakes than I care to. Luckily, I will always have the good memories of those people while they were alive, but I also have that vivid memory of them laying there in that box, not looking anything at all like they looked in life. Therefore, I told her that when my time comes, I don't want people lining up in some sort of warped parade-like procession to stare at my makeup-laden carcass hauntingly lying like some sort of zombiefied clown in a box.

If you have even the slightest inclination to specific final wishes, don't leave it up to your family to guess and question whether or not they made the right decision for the rest of their lives. Just take less than one minute out of the more than thirty-nine million in your lifetime (based on a seventy-five-year life expectancy) to tell someone about your final wishes.

STEP TWO: WHO'S GOING TO PAY FOR ALL THIS?

Typical funeral expenses add up to somewhere between ten thousand and thirty thousand dollars. Tell people how those bills are going to get paid, because the people who perform the services are going to want that settled within thirty days following your death. You don't want to leave this Earth only to force your family to foot the bill for your departure. Make sure your family knows about life insurance, retirement plans, estate plans, and anything else that may help them cover the cost of your final preparations.

There's no such thing as too much information in the New Death Etiquette. If you have life insurance and that's where you want people to draw the necessary funds to pay for your funeral expenses, give them all the information they need. Tell them what the company name is, the contact info, the policy number, who the agent is, and any other information you may have. Any missing piece of information can result in a frustrating experience, so just make sure it's all written down for them somewhere. One small detail missing in each aspect of your final affairs can add up quickly to cause serious unwanted stress, frustration, and wasted time during your loved ones' scavenger hunt.

STEP THREE: WHERE IS EVERYTHING?

The first two steps along the Stairway to Heaven are immediate. Those things need to be thought of and done before your body becomes cold. Step three is a little less urgent, but it takes the longest for your loved ones to accomplish. This is the part of the process where you tell people where all of your *stuff* is.

Start with such big-ticket items as mortgages, cars, personal loans, and any other big financial assets. Nobody is obligated to pay the mortgage of a deceased relative, but it still has to get paid, or the property needs to be sold by somebody. Somebody also needs to know where all the proof-of-ownership documents are. They could be in a safe deposit box or underneath the mattress in your bedroom, or maybe there's a secret passageway behind the wall of your kitchen that's only accessible by removing the plastic apple from the fake fruit bowl on the table. Wherever that *stuff* is, make sure somebody else knows about it.

Then document all the smaller *stuff*, such as credit cards, bank accounts, retirement plans, and any life insurance that's left over after the funeral expenses have been paid off. Filtering down even further, make sure your list of *stuff* or Will contains information on who gets such things as jewelry, tools, artwork, firearms, golf clubs, electronics, and more. If your Will doesn't contain that specific information, then make sure your intentions regarding who should receive those items are clearly spelled out somewhere. Otherwise, you risk extended family battles, where bickering over perceived sentimental value destroys relationships. Death can be a time that brings families closer together or a time of great division. It's really up to us which one will happen. Maybe Dad had a vintage car valued at forty thousand dollars that both boys think they have the right to sole possession of. Or, maybe Mom had some fine china that's only used at holidays, and all the girls in the family swear she told each of them that they should have it when she's gone. If you don't clearly state which boy or girl is supposed to get those items, there's going to be some harsh words, hurt feelings, and long-lasting emotional scars over these things. Additionally, providing a list of your online accounts and how to access them, from bill paying to social media profiles, will save your loved ones an enormous amount of time, stress, and money.

Chapter 5

MAKE IT LEGAL, AND MAKE SURE SOMEBODY KNOWS YOU HAVE IT

"Estate planning is an important and everlasting gift you can give your family. And setting up a smooth inheritance isn't as hard as you might think."

—SUZE ORMAN

A lot of things have changed over the years, but family is still family, and no matter how warm and fuzzy a picture of your family that you currently have, they're going to fight over your *stuff* when you're gone. It's been that way for about three hundred thousand years now. Consider the following prehistoric example:

THE PREHISTORIC TRAGEDY OF THE CAVEMEN BROTHERS UNGA, BUNGA, AND MUNGA

In the early days of man, Munga the caveman would go out hunting for saber-toothed tiger meat with his brothers, Unga and Bunga. After a hearty breakfast of brontosaurus bacon and pterodactyl eggs, this trio headed out for a full day of hunting, each with his own trusty weapon of choice.

Next thing you know, Munga got run over and eaten by a wild stampede of hungry velociraptors. (Yes, I realize that man was never on the Earth at the same time as the dinosaurs. But two guys named Fred and Barney never had aspirations of becoming the Grand Poo-Bah at the Water Buffalo Lodge either. So, work with me.) Our boys had seen the pack of ravenous raptors heading straight for them, but as the old saying goes, Unga and Bunga didn't need to be fast, they just needed to be faster than Munga.

After the dinosaur dust settled, nothing was left of poor Munga for a proper caveman burial. However, his trusty hunting spear, which of course did him no good in this particular situation, was left perfectly untouched. Evidently, raptors had no use for tools. So now Unga and Bunga were left rigorously debating in their Neanderthal manner which one should inherit their unfortunate brother's most cherished weapon.

Instinctively and rather rudely, Unga then proceeded to take his club and smash his brother, Bunga, over the head with it, just as Bunga equally rudely smashed him in the face with a rock. The two of them fell unceremoniously to their sudden deaths beside their dino-fodder brother, and what had started out as just another day at the office ended in total prehistoric tragedy. Hence, nobody got the spear.

Today's battles are fought in the courtroom instead of with clubs, rocks, and spears, but the point is still the same. Just like in ancient history, families will fight over your *stuff*. It could be argued that we handle it in a more civilized manner today, but anyone who has witnessed some of these ugly, drawn-out court battles may contend that a swift bludgeoning over the head with a club would be far less painful than several years of court appearances and family infighting.

The good news is that it doesn't have to be this way. Establish a Will, have a conversation, and let somebody close to you know where all your *stuff* is.

WHEN DOVES CRY

Prince, or the Artist Formerly Known as Prince (given his current state of existence), did not have a Will. That's right: one of the greatest rock 'n' roll icons of all time did not take the time to meet with one of the numerous, readily available attorneys to make a Will. Therefore, the rights to all of his music, both published and unpublished, as well as his entire estate (valued unofficially at a bazillion, gazillion, gargantuillion dollars) is tied up in the courts, and that's exactly where it is likely to stay for the next ten years, *minimum*. People are coming (some particularly smarmy deplorables are crawling) out of the woodwork, claiming their own stake to a portion of his money. There are various female companions, people claiming to be offspring, unknown relatives—you name it—they all want their own piece, and ironically all that his true beneficiaries want is their own peace. Don't do that to your family.

Understandably, you're not Prince. Most likely, your net worth isn't equal to five square feet of the man's shoe closet (I'm sure mine isn't), but you still have *stuff*. It's got some value, and it's going to help your family after you're gone. It's been estimated that only 45 percent of people today have a Will. (I don't buy that statistic. Personally, I would wager good money that it's much less than that.) If you're one of these people who don't have a Will, go out and make one ASAP—especially if you have kids. Don't leave a legacy of unanswered questions!

OPTIONS

It's always better to engage the advice of a professional attorney to put a Will together. They have the experience it takes to sit down face-to-face with you and explain everything that needs to be done. Moreover, they will suggest many alternatives and options, which you have likely never considered before. The most important aspect of this planning is to make certain that what you want to happen actually happens! Furthermore, your *stuff* changes as your life goes on. A good attorney will work with you to update your Will as assorted life changes inevitably take place.

I know you may be thinking, "That's great, Jon, but I simply can't afford to pay attorney fees". Attorneys are great, but they can be somewhat expensive, and not everybody can afford them. In the event you simply cannot or will not hire a professional, there are several good online options, such as LegalZoom and Rocket Lawyer, which can help if cost is a problem. These websites enable you to put your Will, advance directives, and even your own estate plan together without hiring potentially cost-prohibitive legal counsel. A nice option within these services is the ability to purchase the counsel of their legal staff for a discounted rate on top of the DIY Will kit.

BENEFICIARIES

Most people who have a retirement plan, whether it's a good old-fashioned pension—attention millennials: you might need to look up the term *pension* if you've never heard of it before, but believe it or not, they actually used to exist—or the more current 401(k) plan, list their spouse as the primary beneficiary. As long as the beneficiary's name is listed correctly, there is usually an immediate transfer of the benefit upon death. Unfortunately, life moves fast today, and the divorce rate is still at a pretty high clip in America. Make sure you update your beneficiary situation periodically to ensure that an ex-wife or ex-husband doesn't receive your benefit in place of your current spouse. Therefore, making sure your beneficiary information is always kept up-to-date is a must-do. You can't apologize, much less fix it, when you are dead. You would certainly not be leaving a good legacy behind in that case... very poor execution of the New Death Etiquette.

Life insurance is something you can usually list a contingent beneficiary on. In layman's terms, "contingent" means "second in line." In other words, list your spouse as the primary beneficiary, but in the tragic event that something happens to the both of you at the same time, make sure you list someone else who should receive those benefits. More often than not, you may choose to list one of your kids as the contingent beneficiary. But this may be problematic if your children are minors. We'll discuss this in greater detail in the next chapter. The last thing you want is to neglect this technicality, resulting in nobody getting the benefit... again, very poor execution of the New Death Etiquette.

LIFE INSURANCE IS ONLY GOOD IF SOMEBODY KNOWS YOU HAVE IT

Over one billion dollars' worth of life insurance has gone unpaid, because people die all the time without having told anybody else that they actually had it. I'm a firm believer in life insurance because it has so many useful purposes for those who will ultimately receive the benefit—not the least of which is paying for whatever happens to my body when I no longer have a need for it.

As an interesting side note, I once had a woman tell me that she would never buy life insurance because she thought it was bad luck and would jinx her. Wow, I never thought of that. So, if I don't buy life insurance, I guess I'll live forever? After being presented with this logistical paradox, I couldn't help myself, so I asked her if her house had ever burned down or if she had ever been in a car accident. Her answer to both was, "No." Then, I asked if she had fire insurance on her house and automobile insurance on her car. To which, she responded with, "Of course I do." I'll let you think about that for a moment.

So, if you have life insurance, do you really want to keep paying into something like that only to have it go to absolutely nobody after you die, because you procrastinated too much about telling someone about it while you were alive?

This is especially likely to happen if young people are left to pick up the pieces of deceased parents, because young people may not even understand life insurance, and we as parents likely haven't told them about it. Additionally, they may not possess the knowledge that many employers once gave life insurance to their workers as a benefit. Some people, especially many union and government employees have retiree life insurance, meaning their former company picks up the bill, which continues the policy even after retirement. But, none of this helps if you don't tell your beneficiaries about it before it's too late. Therefore, the policy goes unclaimed, and guess what? Insurance companies don't have people on staff that scan the obituaries nationwide every morning to see if any of their policy holders walked into the light. Oddly enough, insurance companies have plenty of staff members who are tracking down receivables, but they're not so eager to find people who need to be paid out.

Make sure that people know where to find any sources of potential claims (money) when you die. Thank God that

Ted was a borderline hoarder. Actually, it's good in some ways and bad in others. It's bad because Michelle and Marie had an overwhelming tower of paperwork, boxes of files, check registers, bank statements, and more to tackle. But, it's good because he kept everything, so eventually we were able to find most of his *stuff*.

Death is hard for the people left behind—much harder than for the people who actually die, which by comparison is relatively easy to accomplish. Usually, the surviving family members find themselves at the funeral home twenty-four hours postmortem with the director telling them that the total cost of the services comes to around sixteen thousand dollars and that payment in full is expected within thirty business days. Ironically, this is usually spoken approximately five seconds after he tells them how sorry he is for their loss. Most folks aren't going to reach into their back pockets at that time and pull out a roll of hundred-dollar bills to hand over. They're going to need to find out where the life insurance is and how to collect it.

RAIDERS OF THE LOST SAFE DEPOSIT BOX

Life insurance and retirement plans aren't the only precious commodities that you need to make sure your family knows about. There could be bank accounts out there and other valuables that you haven't made family members privy to the whereabouts of. For instance, one of the great mysteries left in the aftermath of my father-in-law's passing was a key left in the center desk drawer of his office. We had no idea what the key unlocked. It could have been for the Ark of the Covenant for all we knew. Certainly, if we had found a wide-brimmed fedora and a bullwhip in the closet, we would have needed to investigate the situation with a little more interest. I wonder if Ted had an uncommon fear of snakes. Okay, we knew it was a safe deposit box key but had no idea where the box was located.

Our first thought was to call the Dane County Credit Union, because that's where he did the majority of his banking, but that was a dead end. After over a week and a half of calling various local banks, credit unions, and even chambers of commerce, we finally found a match to a safe deposit box in a bank on the other side of town, where he had absolutely no other accounts.

The moral of the story: make sure someone—your spouse, children, financial advisor, trusted friend, someone—knows where to find all the information about how to access your *stuff*, and who it all rightly belongs to.

Chapter 6

FAMILY DYNAMICS

"No one wants to die. Even people who want to go to heaven don't want to die to get there. And yet death is the destination we all share. No one has ever escaped it. And that is as it should be, because death is very likely the single best invention of life. It is life's change agent. It clears out the old to make way for the new."

—STEVE JOBS

Once in a while as parents, especially of younger children, we all need a little time off. There comes a time in every parent's life when we desperately need to leave the kids for a few days to engage in adult conversation and have a mini-vacation from being a parent. Therefore, we stop by Grandma and Grandpa's house, drop the kids off, run for the car like Olympic sprinters, screech the tires, and get the hell out of Dodge for a few days to decompress. Just before we sprint out the door, however, we usually leave a set of clear and concise instructions for the old folks to properly care for our kids. That list may look a little like this:

- They get two hours of screen time per day—no more, or they will turn into unresponsive, comatose-looking, *Children of the Corn*–type beings, completely incapable of following any sort of command or performing any basic functional task such as eating or sleeping.
- If you want to get any sleep at all, make sure little three-year-old Susie has her Lovie at bedtime every night, because hell hath no fury like Susie sans Lovie at bedtime.
- Limit liquids before bedtime. Obvious middle-of-the-night, laundry-related problems ensue otherwise.
- They need to read for at least thirty minutes per day. The consequence of not adhering to such a simple request results in screen time being taken away, which is a punishment they will do almost anything to avoid.
- No junk food. Okay... sparing amounts of junk food interspersed with actual nutrition is fine. Just don't open a wholesale-club-sized bag of Cool Ranch Doritos and tell them to have at it for dinner.
- Unless ending up in the ER sounds like a fun activity for the weekend, make sure Johnny takes his meds every day and stays away from anything that's ever had a peanut even remotely associated with it.

- Make sure they both eat their vegetables. This one could take a while and often comes down to a battle of wills. Keep an eye on the dog during this confrontation.

That list is likely to go on a lot further. Every kid is different, just like every parent is different, so naturally, the complete and specific list depends on both factors. The point is that we're always so careful to have these discussions with our babysitters even if we're just going out to dinner for a couple of hours on a Saturday night. Why the heck wouldn't you leave equally clear and concise instructions for the potential permanent caretakers of your children?

THE JOB DESCRIPTION OF A PARENT
JOB SUMMARY

Growth-minded, family-run organization seeks strong-willed, independent leader with sharp focus, excellent communication skills, and a tireless work ethic. This individual needs to remain oblivious to any form of emotional trauma and infinitely tolerant of several forms of bad organizational behavior, including name-calling, temper tantrums, and frequently awkward displays of public embarrassment and humiliation.

The qualified candidate must be willing to take on limitless responsibilities and receive little to no gratitude in the process. If you enjoy working in a fast-paced, sleep-deprived, safety-endangering, and endlessly challenging work environment, then this is the role for you.

Holidays require even more work, and sick time is out of the question. In fact, any time off taken without the proper assignment of an equally qualified candidate to serve in the interim will be punished to the full extent of the law. Upon acceptance of this role, you will be committed to fulfilling it to the best of your natural abilities at the expense of your own leisure time and often your physical and mental well-being for the rest of your life—any length of time less than that will be considered unacceptable.

RESPONSIBILITIES & DUTIES

Additional responsibilities include, but are not limited to, the following:

- Perform to optimal levels on little to no actual quality sleep for many years.
- Possess elite project management skills and be capable of keeping rigid schedules and overcoming resistance and objections to adhere to those schedules at all times.

- Be a master chef of such gourmet dishes as macaroni and cheese, chicken nuggets, and endless forms of cheese pizza.
- In addition to unsurpassed leadership abilities, be willing to assume the role of housemaid, wait staff, and chauffer whenever needed.
- Handle various emergency situations with the utmost care and calmness of state of mind.
- Be perceived with complete hatred at various intervals, especially when your subordinates range in age from twelve to eighteen.
- Accept the fact that you will be viewed as a total embarrassment for many years, also especially when your subordinates range in age from twelve to eighteen.
- Screen phone calls and serve as organizational watchdog if various undesirable peers of your subordinates attempt to gain entry to your family's personal life.
- Be on call twenty-four hours per day, seven days a week, with no paid holidays and absolutely no time off.

COMPENSATION

- Nothing. In fact, acceptance of this role may cost you close to three hundred thousand dollars over the course of the next eighteen years or more.

EXPERIENCE REQUIRED

- None necessary. On-the-job training will be provided that makes boot camp in any branch of the military look like an eight-week stay in the Bahamas.

If all this sounds like you, welcome to the club. Start a family today!

To characterize the previous job description of a parent as challenging is an understatement of severe proportions. Think about that when you're selecting a guardian for your kids in the event that something happens to you and your spouse, because this individual damned well better be prepared to fulfill those job responsibilities and then some. Some of us may immediately think about naming our own mom and dad as caretakers, but what if your mom and dad are eighty years old? In a situation like that, there's a good chance that your children will have to go through a displacement process more than once, and nobody wants that.

Therefore, the next thing that we need to think about is who is physically and mentally capable of taking on these sorts of job requirements? After that, who do you think would raise your children in a way compatible with your unique parenting style? Everybody does things differently, especially as parents:

- Some parents are strict, while others are a little more lenient.
- Some parents believe strongly in religion, while others see it as a convenient fairytale.

- Some parents see television as the root of all evil, while others see it as a necessary babysitter for a mandatory couple of hours per day of peace and quiet.
- Some parents prepare only natural and healthy foods for snacks and meals, while others see chicken nuggets as valuable protein, french-fries as a reasonable choice for starch, and ketchup as a vegetable.

Think about all the points of differentiation your kids may have to deal with when you select a legal guardian, because if they're used to a carefree lifestyle of McDonalds and *Three Stooges* marathons, it's going to be awfully hard for them to deal with kale salads and the *National Geographic* channel.

THE CHOSEN ONE

After you narrow down the list of candidates to the chosen one to be the caregiver for your children, have a conversation with that person. Most of the time, if you've thought carefully about who this person should be and made a smart decision, that person will agree to take on the role.

Keep in mind that a designated godparent is not a legally binding arrangement. Many people think that by naming this person with a religious connotation, they are naming a legal guardian for that child. This is 100 percent false. A godparent is not a legally defined role and has no actual impact on end-of-life arrangements. A guardian named in your last Will and testament is the only person legally defined as the chosen one.

CNN Money recently published an article that cited the US Department of Agriculture's annual "Expenditures on Children by Families," which was created in conjunction with FutureAdvisor and which stated that the average cost of raising a child today is approximately $245,000. That's a pretty hefty price tag to place on the chosen one and a very costly faux pas concerning the New Death Etiquette. Therefore, establishing a trust following your death, funded by life insurance or whatever other means possible, is strongly recommended. This legal trust is what will help to offset the cost of raising your child. Maybe your child goes to private school, and your legal guardians can't afford that. A legal trust funded by your life insurance could help to continue paying for it. This is why having an attorney is critical in establishing your plans.

Maybe you have a half-million dollars in life insurance that can be tapped for any future expenses. The legal guardian would become the trustee, who would access those funds for various items that are clearly defined within the trust for your child's various needs, including emergencies, college, healthcare, and more. If you don't establish a trust ahead of time, that's okay too; as long as you define legal guardianship in your Will, then a testamentary trust is established after your death. The process may encounter a little more red tape and last a bit longer than what is ideal. For added context about how detrimental and disruptive not having a Will can be to your children, consider this story from an estate-planning attorney friend of mine.

A couple in their mid-thirties left their children with a babysitter one night to have a dinner date that they sorely needed. Unfortunately, fate intervened in a horrific way when they were struck head-on by another vehicle on the highway and killed almost instantly. Adding to the tragedy is the fact that the children were only three and five years old.

It gets worse. The couple had also not done any estate planning at all. And who could really blame them? They were young and healthy as far as they knew. Nobody could have predicted the cruel twist of fate they encountered, which is precisely why you need to be prepared at any age, especially if you have children.

Because there was no Will, within a week, the in-fighting among family members already began, especially concerning the kids. In the short term, the wife's parents took in the children and cared for them. That's when the real difficulties began though, because shortly after, the husband's parents, who lived in another state, decided that they wanted to be named legal guardians.

Since no legal document existed that formally announced who should be the legal guardians, the case was taken to probate court. That's when a judge had to decide where the kids would go. So, in this case, not taking the five minutes it would have required to name legal guardians resulted in a judge deciding who would raise these very young children, instead of their parents. The process of deciding who would be named didn't even begin until three months after the tragedy occurred. In the interim, the kids got shuffled back and forth between grandparents and various aunts and uncles on a weekly basis, until a permanent guardian was formally named.

OF UTMA-OST IMPORTANCE

The Uniform Transfer to Minors Act (UTMA) dictates that a minor may receive a gift of money from a donor, but a custodian will be named, who will be in complete control and management of the account. In other words, you can't leave a quarter of a million dollars to your six-year-old daughter so she can spend it on gummy bears and Calico Critters in a futile effort to help her grieve your loss. Therefore, even if you have a Will and you name your son or daughter as the beneficiaries on life insurance policies, make sure you designate a responsible party to take over guardianship and custodial duties of your kids, a party who also has the wherewithal to responsibly manage their inheritance.

If you don't specify who takes guardianship of your kids, you're asking for serious trouble. There will undoubtedly be bickering and lifelong, relationship-killing resentment among family members who all think they can do a better job of raising your kids. Aunts and uncles, godparents, and even various close friends of the family will get caught up in trying to take control. You'll be leaving the fate of your children up to the courts to decide, which may not be the ideal situation. This process could take years to properly resolve in our overbooked court system, leaving your children with literally no place to truly call home in the meantime.

NOW WHAT?

In a different story from an estate-planning attorney I know, there's another valuable lesson in the New Death Etiquette. It's about a couple in their mid-forties with two children, ages nine and eleven.

The husband had no previous health issues that anyone knew about, but one fateful evening, he woke up clutching his chest. Unfortunately, he died before the ambulance could even get to the house. Like a lot of couples, the husband and wife each had their own clearly defined roles. The wife took care of the kids and maintained the order of the house, while the husband had worked and maintained the finances. Certainly, that's not the case with a lot of families these days, but that just happened to be the way this family dynamic worked. The problem with this arrangement was that when the husband died, the wife had no idea how to handle any of the finances. She wasn't prepared to answer any of the following questions from the kids:

- Will we have to move out of our house?
- Can we still go to college someday?
- Do we have enough money without Dad?
- Will we have to give up our car?

She would have loved to provide her kids with some parental reassurance, but she just didn't have any of those answers, because she didn't know where any of the assets were. At a time when the family should have been focused on caring for one another and grieving together, they were instead consumed with fear and uncertainty. They had no idea where the next dollar was coming from, and they were understandably scared.

The attorney entered the situation because the wife had to enlist his firm's services to find out where some of the couple's accounts were. His firm had to write letters to each of the financial institutions within the area and find out if the couple had an account there. The search included banks, credit unions, life insurance companies, and much more. It was a time-consuming and expensive process.

In fact, by the time such a search is completed, you'd better hope the life insurance is enough to cover the cost of the legal bills involved. The saddest part is that it doesn't have to be that way. If you just write down where this *stuff* is and have a discussion, you can stop this sort of thing from happening to your family.

WHAT ABOUT THE FUR BABIES?

Whether it's a dog, a cat, a potbellied pig, or a hamster, many people treat their fur babies as family members. This notion isn't just limited to people without kids either. There are plenty of households with three, four, and five children that still treat their pets like a furrier, smellier, but fully lovable member of the family, and their ongoing care is a very important final wish to consider. With this in mind, consider including your fur baby in your Will to ensure that it will be properly cared for beyond your life.

If nobody steps up, a dog is likely to find its way to the shelter, and who knows what happens from there.

The first thing you need to think about is who you want to care for the pet after you're gone. In some cases, family members may be so disenchanted with each other that not only do they fight over Mom's valuable jewelry, but they also fight over every other small and seemingly inconsequential thing, such as her pet guinea pig, Mr. Whiskers. Hopefully, this isn't the case, but be aware of the possibility of this level of pettiness, just in case. This is another instance where updating your Will is important because the life of an average golden retriever is only somewhere between twelve and fifteen years, and you want to make sure you're not leaving instructions to feed a four-pound Chihuahua named Nacho the amount of food you gave seven years ago to your two-hundred-pound ill-tempered bull mastiff named Sasquatch. That could get ugly really fast.

A guinea pig like Mr. Whiskers or even Nacho the Chihuahua probably won't require much of a financial investment for whoever takes over his care, but if someone inherits a beast like Sasquatch, that situation is going to require some money for upkeep. His food alone might cost close to a thousand dollars per year. And veterinarians aren't exactly cheap these days. Sasquatch is still going to need shots and occasional wellness visits. Therefore, the right thing to do is to leave a little bit of money aside for someone who is willing to take over the responsibility of your fur baby's tender loving care. Multiply the annual cost of food, health, and care costs by the number of years remaining in the critter's life expectancy, and dedicate that amount from your estate plan to the pet's caregiver.

Be very specific in your instructions to the caregiver of your fur baby too. Don't just say Sasquatch needs to eat three times a day and be let outside every three to four hours to do his business—get specific:

- Is Sasquatch a gentle giant, or does he require military-grade body armor and an electric cattle prod when handling him?
- Does Sasquatch sleep through anything, or does he require gentle reassurance and a soft lullaby during thunderstorms and other typically anxiety-causing situations for most dogs?
- Assuming his diet doesn't consist of small goats and unsuspecting mail carriers, what does he eat? Some people are horrified by the mere thought of canned Alpo for their dogs. If the dog has been eating Science Diet his whole life, then you want to continue that routine. Some people—my grandmother, for one—cooked actual meals for her dogs, consisting of beef, chicken and rice.
- How do you brush Sasquatch's fur? (Other than the obvious, which is very carefully.)
- Who is his vet?

- Is he on any medications?
- Does he have a favorite blanket or dog bed that he can't sleep without?

My grandmother had dogs for virtually her entire life—mostly beagles, because she especially loved that breed. She had four of them at one point while I was growing up. The last one died when I was in my twenties and my grandmother was in her eighties. I remember asking her if she was going to get another dog, and she told me, "I can't get another pet, because it will outlive me." She was carrying out the New Death Etiquette without even being aware of it, because she was thoughtfully considering what would happen to a new pet. It turns out that she was right, because she died about five years later.

THE NEW DEATH ETIQUETTE FOR ONE

The New Death Etiquette doesn't apply to just married couples or partners and families. It applies to everybody, even those living alone. You don't want to be the single, elderly woman living alone with twenty-seven cats whose body gets discovered three weeks postmortem by the nice lady next door because a strange smell was emanating from the residence.

If you live alone, maintain a community that periodically checks on your well-being. Just let a neighbor, a fellow churchgoer, or a close acquaintance know that if they see a few newspapers start to pile up in the driveway and they haven't heard from you in a while, knock on the door or call on the phone—do something just to make sure that you and your twenty-seven neglected cats aren't the source of that strange smell.

People with elderly parents need to be especially aware of this. My mother-in-law, Marie, is eighty-seven years old as of now, and she's effectively living alone. Life expectancy is less than eighty-seven, so what happens if she falls and can't get up? Luckily, there are systems in place for just this circumstance now, such as Life Alert, which is the source of that classic television commercial that became such an iconic piece of Americana: "I've fallen, and I can't get up!"

Beyond Life Alert, there are other systems that can be put in place today. State-of-the-art security systems involve a combination of webcams and motion sensors that are effective for not only keeping intruders out but also ensuring the well-being of an elderly loved one. You can set one of them up so that when someone enters a certain area, such as the kitchen or a stairway, the motion detectors are activated and you can see this activity from your smartphone. If that detector at the bottom of the stairs usually goes off at eight every morning when your grandparent gets up to make coffee, but it doesn't go off one day for some reason, you know you need to make a phone call. The security system as a wellness check is an excellent way of using recent technology to keep an eye on the health of your elderly loved one even if you live across the country.

Everyone and everything needs to be considered in the New Death Etiquette. Grandparents, parents, children, spouses, pets, and all the physical and emotional things that tie them all together require preparation for the day you will no longer be with them.

Chapter 7

YOUR DIGITAL LIFE CONTINUES WITHOUT YOU

"Privacy is dead, and social media is holding the smoking gun."

—PETE CASHMORE, MASHABLE CEO

Your digital life continues interminably past the expiration of your physical body. Sure, your lifeless corpse isn't posting, tweeting, snapping, twerking, or updating your status anymore. You're not changing your relationship status from "It's complicated" to "I'm dead," but your friends, relatives, and various other assorted followers can continue addressing your social media account through their own profiles. We've already mentioned the necessity for someone to call your old friends and acquaintances when you die, but who will disable those constantly buzzing social media accounts for you after you're gone? Who will manage the cavalcade of digital interactions for you when you die? Luckily, Facebook is a bit ahead of the curve in this area.

CESAR'S STORY

Although Facebook is at the forefront of allowing people to pull the plug on your digital life when the time comes, it's only possible if you do the right thing and name a legacy contact prior to your passing. Consider the following story from an acquaintance of mine, named Cesar, who had bigger things to worry about besides disabling someone's Facebook account, but it's one little thing that could have been made easier while he was caring for so many larger things.

Cesar is a young guy, in his thirties, with a wife and two kids. His mother-in-law was sadly killed in a car accident in November of 2015. It was a tragic incident that left her family shocked and grieving for a long time after. Unfortunately, it also left them scrambling to pick up the pieces of her end-of-life affairs with no direction because she had not made a plan of any kind.

It's been over a year and a half now since the untimely passing of Cesar's mother-in-law, and because she had not organized her life in any way, multiple family members were in disagreement over her *stuff*. Cesar has most of her possessions kept in his garage, where he's no longer able to park his cars because it's chock-full of *stuff* now. He's also spending an inordinate amount of time trying to sort who should get what and the many repercussions that will follow based on who feels cheated from it. Some things also have to be sold and put in different locations, so there's an added item for Cesar's to-do list that he didn't need. The last time I spoke with Cesar, he had just received permission from Facebook to disable her Facebook account. After many battles, it was just one small victory in a war of bureaucratic inefficiencies. I'm not even sure how many phone calls and emails it took Cesar to win this battle, but it certainly didn't happen right away either.

THE SOCIAL MEDIA MEMORIAL

One of the things that would have made Cesar's life a little easier would have been if his mother-in-law left him as her legacy contact. Then, he would have been able to at least manage or disable that just by submitting a death certificate. To name a legacy contact, execute the following simple, step-by-step process:

1. Go to your Facebook profile page.
2. Click **Settings**, **Security**, **Legacy Contact**, and **Edit**.
3. Type the name of your legacy contact.
4. Click **Add**.
5. Choose either (1) **Send** to alert them with a message that they have been named as your legacy contact, or (2) **Not Now** to not send them anything.

Your survivor can also memorialize a Facebook account without being designated as a legacy contact, but they still need to provide proof of death. A memorialized Facebook account includes the word "Remembering" before the name and will not be included in "People You May Know," Facebook ads, or birthday reminders.

By properly disabling or memorializing your social media account after your death, your survivor is saving your friends and acquaintances around the world the embarrassment of posting something potentially insensitive to your account. To amplify this point, during the final editing process for this book, I received a notification on my LinkedIn account to wish "Happy birthday" to a longtime business associate named Pete. The problem is that Pete passed away about three years ago! I'm hopeful that his other five hundred plus connections also know that Pete is no longer replying "Thank you for the birthday wishes" from his account.

If you are a legacy contact of a deceased person's Facebook account or any other social media accounts, I would recommend that you access their account, disable posts, and write something like an obituary. You can let people know such details as when and where the service is, and you don't have to disable posting if you don't want to. Another option is to leave it open for a year or two so that friends can post about happy times and pleasant memories of the person you're memorializing. You're still in control of the page, so if someone posts something that you don't approve of, you can always delete it.

AUTOPAY EQUALS AUTOPAIN

There are other online activities to consider regarding the New Death Etiquette. For instance, who will stop your automatic subscription renewal to the *Wall Street Journal* on your iPad? For example, I read two newspapers every day: The *Wall Street Journal* and the *Wisconsin State Journal*. (Oddly enough, both use the abbreviation WSJ.) Both of these publications collect a recurring online subscription fee that automatically renews from my credit card. Michelle has no interest in reading either one of them, because she views it as news that is never good anymore, and she's probably right about that. If something happened to me where she needed to discontinue that subscription, it's likely that she would need to call the credit card company to stop the fee, which likely would have processed several times prior to her realizing it was still being collected. Furthermore, unless she's authorized on the account, the credit card companies get a little stubborn about that sort of request. The easier scenario would be to just go into my iPad and turn off the autopay feature. The problem with that option is that my iPad unlocks automatically with my thumbprint or a password, and what if she doesn't know or remember the password?

Online magazine and newspaper subscriptions aren't the only thing you might be using autopay for these days, either. There's Netflix for binge-watching all the episodes of *Gilmore Girls* you can possibly handle, Keurig for productivity-based caffeine addiction, Blue Apron if you have an appreciation for good food but a disdain for going to the grocery store, Hulu for anything Netflix doesn't cover, Amazon Prime to give you unlimited free shipping on just about any shopping item in the known universe, and many more. You might have several of these going on a continual basis that could easily amount to hundreds of dollars per month in autopay fees for online usage that your spouse or children may not want or need. Write down your passwords to your devices and your subscriptions so your family doesn't have to continue paying for the monthly subscription fee for such things as the Cigar of the Month Club. There are even apps such as

Dashlane or 1Password that enable you to record your passwords to everything. Of course, just remember to leave the password to your device with Dashlane or 1Password on it somewhere else.

ICLOUDY WITH A CHANCE OF LOCKOUT

You've no doubt had the experience of returning from work after a two-week vacation in a sunny locale to sit in front of your computer at the login screen, unable to remember what your password was before you left. It's a brain fart of epic proportions, and it happens virtually every year, yet you still don't write down your login info somewhere before you leave. After thoroughly beating yourself up over this repeatedly stupid behavior, you get three cracks at the password, and then comes that fateful lockout message that makes you feel like you're some sort of cybercriminal being denied access to conduct your malicious experiments. The good news is that all you need to do is call the help desk, and they can reset your password for you with proper personal identification. The bad news is that the condescending know-it-alls at the help desk are going to be a royal pain in the ass about it, and at that point, you're going to wish you were actually dead. Nonetheless, it's going to get done, and you will have access at some point, sooner rather than later. Ironically, it's not that simple when trying to access your personal iPhone or iPad, so you can watch unlimited YouTube videos of cats behaving like people and babies versus puppies in a cuteness showdown.

How will anyone even know how to access my iPad? It's set to unlock with my thumbprint. Does that mean someone is going to have to find my cold, dead body to place my thumb on the home button of my iPad just to unlock it? (That seems a little disrespectful to the dead.) Maybe a whole new industry of dead-guy's-thumb-cutting professionals will be spawned from this—something like "the End-of-Life Thumbprint Delivery Service." I can just see them showing up at the funeral home with a razor-sharp slicing device like a cigar cutter to snip off the thumb of the deceased, and then deliver it in a commercially branded storage container to the deceased's home for iPad access. I'm probably not the only one warped enough to think of something like this. Perhaps someone like Elon Musk or Richard Branson has already anticipated it, or maybe it will be featured in the next Michael Bay sci-fi explode-a-fest, *Thumb Cutters* (rated R). Naturally, my iPad can be unlocked using a code, but of course the whole thumb scenario would probably be easier, unless I let someone know what that code is.

If you have an iCloud account and neglect to mention what your password is to that account, your spouse may need to enlist the services of the hackers from the program *Mr. Robot* in order to unlock that thing, because your ordinary, run-of-the-mill computer geek living in his mother's basement, eating Cheetos, and playing PlayStation, isn't going to be able to do it.

To accentuate this point, another attorney told me the story of a man whose widow tried to access his iCloud account, where he had stored some valuable financial information. Unfortunately, she didn't know his password, and Apple wouldn't even speak with her about it. In fact, not even a death certificate was good enough for them. Turns out, it's plenty enough to collect such things as pension benefits but not to access someone's tablet. She was actually forced to obtain a court order before she could get any information at all. It caused several months of delay and significant loss, just because her husband never took the two and a half seconds to say, "Hey babe, if something happens to me, or if I'm kidnapped by the Russian mafia and held for a ludicrous ransom, you don't need to pay it, but here's my iCloud password just in case."

IT'S THE LITTLE THINGS THAT KILL

In the end, is it the worst thing in the world to have an open Facebook account out there of someone who has passed away? The answer is no, but it's the little things like it that add up to a big unnecessary pain in the ass, especially for your elderly mother-in-law or father, who may not have the stamina to make a gaggle of phone calls every day and chase this *stuff* down. Plus, for the people who are left behind, these things all serve as these nagging little details and painful reminders of your loss. People don't usually realize how big of a problem the totality of these little things are until they go through it. That's when they realize that if only you, the dearly departed, had given them a few key pieces of information, their lives would have been a heck of a lot easier, and they would have been able to properly grieve and move on much more quickly.

Chapter 8

NO ONE GETS OUT OF HERE ALIVE

"My husband wanted to be cremated. I told him I'd scatter his ashes at Neiman Marcus— that way, I'd visit him every day."

—JOAN RIVERS

It's true that no one gets out of here alive, but by leaving clear advance directives for your final wishes, you can at least have a say in how you depart. Think about such things as declaring a healthcare power of attorney (POA) and filling out a Living Will.

Name someone you trust—your spouse, or maybe the child you see as most responsible—to become your healthcare POA. This child should be the one who went to the library on Saturday nights and graduated with honors, not the one who set the school record for keg stands at his fraternity during freshman year. The POA will be legally responsible for making healthcare decisions, including necessary medical treatment, surgical procedures, and various other diagnostic services in the event that you have been declared incapacitated and legally incapable of making such decisions for yourself.

The Living Will is a comprehensive document that states whether or not you want to be kept alive by artificial life-support systems. There are usually three conditions that must be met to carry out the execution of a Living Will:

- An incurable and irreversible condition that will result in your death within a relatively short time unless you are administered life-sustaining treatment
- An irreversible coma
- A persistent vegetative state

You can also choose whether or not you want to be an organ donor, whether or not you want to receive pain medication, and whether or not you want to get food and water if you're in one of the preceding conditions. Not having this document is particularly shortsighted, because you can prepare one easily online in about five minutes today for short money, or at an attorney's office for a little more money but with a little more professional advice and personalization. The most relevant and groundbreaking situation that underlines the urgency of this matter is probably the Terri Schiavo case from 1990.

THE DEFINING MOMENT FOR THE RIGHT-TO-DIE ADVOCACY

Terri Schiavo was only twenty-six years old when she suffered a massive heart attack in the hallway of her own apartment in St. Petersburg, Florida. Her husband, Michael, called 911 immediately after he discovered her that day, but sadly, Terri had already incurred significant brain damage from a lack of sufficient oxygen to her brain by the time the paramedics got there and resuscitated her. She entered a coma and remained in a persistent vegetative state for the next fifteen years.

Many experimental procedures were attempted in the first several years of Terri's vegetative state. It was clear that her loved ones all desperately wanted Terri to come back to them, because they tried just about everything they could to raise her awareness back to a conscious level, but nothing worked. Finally, in 1998, Michael petitioned the court to have Terri's feeding tube removed, because he said that Terri would not have wanted prolonged life support without the realistic hope of recovery. Her parents, however, argued differently. What ensued was an ugly, drawn-out court battle for the next seven years, which was emotionally painful for both sides. In total, fourteen appeals, five lawsuits, and numerous other motions, petitions, and hearings, escalating all the way up to the US Supreme Court and even then-President George W. Bush, were filed and argued until the final appeal was upheld to enact her husband's wishes in March 2005.

A sad story for sure, but even sadder that it all could have been avoided had Terri just filled out a Living Will or even just named a healthcare POA at some point during her young life. Albeit, these were not as common then as they are today, it is a valuable lesson from which we can all learn. Certainly, at age twenty-six, it hardly seems a pressing matter to sign such seemingly morbid legal documentation, but nobody knows what the future holds. Shout out to the millennials who still think death is just for old people! Life is full of the unexpected, and sometimes that unexpected circumstance unfortunately involves tragedy, and you should be prepared for it—not necessarily for your own benefit, but for the ongoing lives and well-being of those around you who love and care for you the most. Nobody needs to dwell on this. In fact, I recommend just the opposite: live your life footloose and fancy free. Get the legal mumbo jumbo of boring paperwork out of the way so you never have to think about it again. Just think of signing this documentation as a minor inconvenience in the course of one of your days, just like any other. Get them signed, out of the way, and move on with your life. There's no need to stretch it out any further or make any bigger an issue out of it than that.

The right to die has since evolved as an issue, extending to the terminally ill as well as the medically unresponsive. Presently, five states, including California, Colorado, Oregon, Vermont, and Washington, have legalized physician aid-in-dying (PAD). Likewise, Washington, DC, has legalized physician assisted suicide via legislation, and Montana has physician assisted suicide via court ruling. I'm unsure if other states will soon follow suit or not, but the issue is definitely a hot-button topic for voters nationwide to maintain awareness of. Consider the following case of another young woman, full of courage and definitely thoughtfully prepared for her own passing.

Brittany Maynard was married just two years before getting a terminal diagnosis of stage-four brain cancer. At the time, California was not a PAD state, so Brittany decided to move across the border to Oregon, where she could choose the day she would end her own life through medically assisted means. It's since been referred to as "death with dignity" and serves to remind us that death isn't just brought about by Father Time. It's something that can occur at far too young an age, and it doesn't always happen from a tragic event such as a car crash. Brittany Maynard was originally diagnosed with brain cancer on New Year's Day 2014. She was only twenty-eight years old, and she died ten months later with her husband at her bedside, holding her hand as she passed.

Declaring final directives for end-of-life care and following death preferences in a clear, legally binding manner is especially important for people with more than one child, because it's strange how often brothers and sisters see the same issue in a completely different light. Political and religious views can vary widely within the same family, as well as many other issues, such as environmentalism, corporate ethics, athletics, and even end-of-life issues. One child may think that Dad always wanted to be cremated with no service other than a big party celebrating his life, while the other may be certain that Dad wanted a proper Christian ceremony with a wake and graveside services. Who gets the right to choose? If you don't leave instructions and fill out a healthcare POA or Living Will, it could kick off a litany of litigation and family bickering over your end-of-life wishes.

Everyone has their own beliefs about quality of life, religious purpose, and family commitment, and we need to respect everyone's individual beliefs, because the other side of the coin is also true. There are plenty of people out there who believe that under no circumstances do they want the plug to be pulled on their life support—some for religious reasons and others who purely believe that this life we live is literally all there is and ever will be, so they don't want to miss out on even one unconscious moment. Whatever your preference is doesn't really matter. What does matter is that you tell someone about it and have it recorded somewhere in a legally binding document so people—especially your family—won't fight over it for years and harbor ill will toward one another for the rest of their living days.

The trouble is you Think you have time.

Chapter 9

FINAL, HAPPY THOUGHTS

"I know not why there is such a melancholy feeling attached to the remembrance of past happiness, except that we fear that the future can have nothing so bright as the past."

—JULIA WARD HOWE, AMERICAN POET AND AUTHOR

What is the legacy you want to leave behind? Do you want people to say something like, "Jon was actually a selfish, self-centered son of a bitch?" Or, do you want them to say something like, "Jon was a really caring guy. Everybody knows he was an avid golfer and hiker, and he loved Arizona. But, how many people know how much he cared for people with autism, and how he would do anything for a friend?" Let's go through a little exercise:

> Close your eyes. Imagine it's a sunny day with a warm, gentle breeze rustling through the clear blue sky with nary a cloud in sight. You're in a church during a ceremony, and people are talking all around you. Some of them are crying, and at that moment you realize you're at a funeral.
>
> Now you realize it's your funeral, and you're the one in the box that everybody is talking about. Eavesdropping was always an undersold talent of yours, so you're listening to the various conversations floating around the room. Some of them are being had by family members, and others by close friends. Still others are being held by mere acquaintances. What do you hope people are saying about you?

LETTERS FROM HEAVEN

Probe deeply into this question. The New Death Etiquette is about more than just getting your shit together. It's an all-encompassing subject about your end-of-life preparation and the legacy you leave behind. While performing the preceding exercise, and thinking about what you hope people will be saying about you, think about leaving a final note for your loved ones as well. Ask yourself this question, "If I knew I wouldn't be here tomorrow, what would I say to my spouse, children, friends, and others today?" It might be something like the following:

I'm gone, and I know you're upset about it. But it's going to be okay. I'm always going to be with you in your heart. You're not alone, because my spirit is still with you; it has been since the day you were born, and it's never going away. We've been through a lot together, and I know you're going to make the right decisions when it really counts. Even if and when you step in a mess, just clean it off your shoe and keep moving forward. Don't look back. It doesn't do any good. You'll be great, and I love you.

The script varies depending on your particular relationship, but it's a chance to tell your children that you simply did the best you could. Tell them how important they were to you and how everything you did with them was out of love. Then you can give them some final words of wisdom: Tell them not to dwell on the past because regret is counterproductive. Tell them to move forward with their lives, because you believe in their ability to do good things. If you're lucky enough to live another twenty-five years or more after you write this letter, you can always change it later on if you need to.

THE POWER OF VIDEO

Perhaps the only thing that could be more effective than writing a heartfelt letter to your loved ones would be a video message. Video is such a powerful tool. It only adds to the effectiveness if your spouse and kids can see your face one last time with those final words of wisdom. They get to see the emotion on your expression and read your body language. It becomes much more impactful, and today's technology, with smartphones, tablets, and selfie sticks, makes it very easy to shoot such a video and keep it archived in your cloud somewhere.

Video is also a good option to spell out some of the minor things you want to leave behind for certain people. If you don't want to use your Will to spell out who gets your golf clubs, cookware, Beanie Baby collection, and other forms of minutiae you collected over your lifetime, then use video to tell everyone who you want to have all this *stuff.*

ESTABLISH OR CHANGE YOUR LEGACY

You writing a letter or filming a video for your loved ones is also a great opportunity for you to change certain things about your legacy if you feel you're not living up to what you're writing. In other words, if you feel like you're traveling too much for work, maybe your writing that down will inspire you to travel less if that is at all possible. Maybe there are other instances of regret that this exercise will force you to think about. That reflection can change your life—and ultimately your legacy—for the better.

JUST DO IT!

After thinking about such things as the scavenger hunt; the caveman trio of Unga, Bunga, and Munga; my friend Nick; my father-in-law, Ted; my uncle Rob; George Carlin's *stuff*; the million and one tentacles of your digital life; and all the other things discussed in this book—are you thoughtfully prepared for the inevitable? Are you adhering to loving, caring, and smart implementation of the New Death Etiquette?

My family isn't any different from the others who span the countryside of this great land or even those that dot the global economy. We have normal relationships in which people put things off, forget about things, and fight over *stuff*—sound familiar? I witnessed firsthand what it was like for my wife and best friend, Michelle, to handle the yearlong challenge of the aftermath from her father's passing. That experience inspired me to create the *My Life and Wishes Organizer* and subsequently an online service, which has since helped countless individuals get their lives in order, digitally and otherwise. So, in a weird way, I do have the unique ability to predict the future of what things will be like for your family after you're gone, but you have the ability to prove me wrong and change it, so do it! Whether you use my organizer, online service, or scribble all the necessary information on a napkin stored in a lockbox in the garage—it doesn't matter—just do it, and in the process, secure an invaluable peace of mind. Also, don't forget, it's only death, so relax and happy planning!

APPENDIX: RESOURCES

If you'd like a professionally structured, organized, secure, and infinitely changeable way of making thoughtful preparations for you and your loved ones, then the *My Life and Wishes* service is a great choice!

Go to MyLifeandWishes.com and enter the coupon code CLICKHERE for 20 percent off for one year of our service.

For information on online Wills and other legal services, check out:

http://www.legalzoom.com
http://www.rocketlawyer.com

For state-by-state downloadable forms and information regarding healthcare advance directives, check out:

http://www.caringinfo.org

THE NEW DEATH ETIQUETTE CHECKLIST

MUST DO

☐ Tell someone you trust—your spouse, your most responsible child, a trusted friend, or legal representative—where to find your *stuff*, in particular the location of a document that clearly tells people what to do and where to go for it all.

☐ Provide as much information as possible regarding financial accounts, such as life insurance policy numbers and beneficiaries, bank account numbers, safe deposit box locations, and so on.

☐ Make your funeral wishes known (burial or cremation, wake or no wake, etc.)

☐ State healthcare advance directives so you have a voice when you can no longer speak.

☐ Name a healthcare POA.

☐ Periodically update your beneficiary information.

☐ Create a list of all online accounts, social and otherwise, including user names, passwords, and challenge questions.

☐ Make a plan to close your social media accounts.

SHOULD DO

☐ Create a Will (move this one to the "Must Do" category if you have children).

☐ Create a trust for your minor children.

☐ Periodically review your Will and beneficiary information.

☐ Create a list of things you own and expenses.

☐ Make a list of causes and charities you wish to donate to after your passing.

☐ Consider long-term-care options.

☐ Preplan for funeral and memorial services.

ABOUT THE
AUTHOR

JON BRADDOCK is an entrepreneur, speaker, and the author of *Advisor or Vendor* and *RetireEase*. He has served as President and CEO of ISG Advisors and has more than thirty years of experience in employee benefit and retirement planning consulting. He and his wife, Michelle, cofounded and currently operate the online digital planning platform MyLifeandWishes.com, which assists people in getting their digital house in order. They live with their children in Madison, Wisconsin.

Made in the USA
Columbia, SC
14 February 2023

12159602R00075